THE UNOFFICIAL
SEAN CONNERY

THE UNOFFICIAL

Sean Connery

BY
Rachel Simpson

· PARRAGON ·

This edition first published by
Parragon Book Service Ltd in 1996

Parragon Book Service Ltd
Unit 13–17 Avonbridge Trading Estate
Atlantic Road, Avonmouth
Bristol BS11 9QD

Produced by Magpie Books,
an imprint of Robinson Publishing

ISBN 0 75251 795 3

A copy of the British Library Cataloguing in Publication
Data is available from the British Library.

Typeset by Whitelaw & Palmer Ltd, Glasgow

THE BOY FROM THE TENEMENTS

Hooray for the world's sexiest old-age pensioner: Sean Connery. Although he turned 65 in August 1995, he's still making films, still collecting awards, and still – many of his female fans would argue – worthy of the accolade 'the sexiest man alive'.

'Well, you don't see many sexy dead men,' he famously quipped when he heard he had been given this title by America's *People* magazine in 1990. True. But there are few men like Connery either: a child of the Edinburgh slums who rose to become a multi-millionaire film star.

Connery was the first – and to many people is still the definitive – James Bond. His career spans 60 films in 40 years. But even though he has won at Oscar along the way, mixed with Royalty, and counts some of the biggest names in show business among his friends, one of Connery's greatest pleasures is still a very simple one – stretching out in a nice hot bath.

Thomas Sean Connery was born on 25 August 1930 in an area of Edinburgh known as Fountainbridge, and hot baths were a rare luxury. The name Fountainbridge may conjure

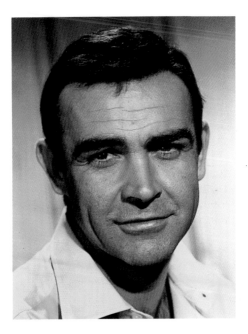

Sean Connery

up visions of fast-flowing rivers and graceful bridges, but in the 1930s it was a land of tenements: tall, forbidding blocks of flats, in streets where the smells from the local brewery and rubber factory filled the air. The only pleasant smell was from the nearby sweet factory.

The two-room apartment which was Sean Connery's first home was cramped, cold and damp, with only the most basic of facilities. There were gas mantles on the walls, and just one toilet, which the Connerys had to share with the family next door. There was no hot water or bathroom, so Connery's adored mother Effie – nobody called her by her full name, Euphamia – kept a tin bath in the yard outside their flat. Throughout his childhood, when young Tommy needed a wash, she would have to lug it in, and heat kettles of water on the cooking stove to fill it up. As he grew older, Tommy would sometimes go to the municipal 'plunge', the public bath house. The amount one paid, 3d, 6d or a whole shilling, determined how much water one could luxuriate in.

The family in which Tommy – as he was then called – grew up, was not well off. 'We were poor, but I never knew *how* poor,' the adult Connery would later say. He was the first child of the family but there was no money for a cot, so 20-year-old Effie improvised and used the bottom drawer of the wardrobe for the new baby to sleep in.

Connery's father Joe was an unskilled labourer, who sometimes also worked as a van driver or porter. He brought home just a few shillings a week in his pay packet. This was the era of the Depression, and there were occasions when Joe couldn't find work; when money was especially tight Tommy would sometimes be sent round the corner to a local pawnshop, to sell an unwanted garment for sixpence or sevenpence. He was very proud of himself on the occasions when he managed to squeeze an extra halfpence out of the shop owner. Even so, the Connerys had to make economies: they would sometimes sit in their kitchen/sitting room in the evening with the lights off to save pennies.

By the time Tommy was 11, and old enough to go to Darroch Secondary School, his mother had found a job cleaning houses in Edinburgh. They needed the money as by now there was another mouth to feed: that of

Tommy's younger brother Neil, born when Tommy was eight. Tommy started looking for ways to bring in a bit of extra cash too. Soon, he was getting up at 5 a.m. even on the darkest, coldest mornings to help deliver milk for the local dairy, St. Cuthbert's. It was there that Tommy Connery first discovered his love of horses: he adored working with the animals who pulled the milk carts. By a strange quirk of fate, one of the places he delivered milk to was Fettes College, the elite school from which James Bond was meant to have been expelled.

Delivering milk wasn't Tommy's only job. In the early evenings, he also helped out the local butcher and coalman. Some of the money earned went into Tommy's own pocket, but his mother put most of it into a Post Office account for him. Sometimes, he used it to see films at the local cinema, the Blue Halls. Adults regarded it as a fleapit where you really did run a risk of coming away with fleas. But Tommy didn't mind. He would watch the 'Flash Gordon' serials eagerly, but what he really enjoyed were traditional Westerns.

Tommy began to grow into a tall teenager and his sprouting muscles and tough attitude gave him the nickname 'Big Tam'. Although he wasn't as rough as some of the other kids, he was tough when he needed to be. One playground fight with a boy named Anderson went to 12 rounds.

Kids grew up fast in Fountainbridge during the 1930s and 1940s, and Tommy Connery was no exception. In 1943, still aged only 13, he left Darroch Secondary School. Perhaps unsurprisingly, Tommy had never really taken to the school, a strict institution where the teachers were only too ready to use the rod on any child who uttered a word out of place, although he enjoyed reading books. He went to work full time at the dairy, determined to get on in the world by earning a living.

He also began to notice girls. Indeed, he couldn't really help but do so when, at the age of 14, he was picked up by a woman from the ATS (the Auxiliary Territorial Service). She took him into a water-logged air-raid shelter, and after removing both their clothes, instructed him in the most essential facts of life. 'I couldn't believe my luck,' he would say afterwards.

During the war years, of course, a lot of soldiers engaged in illicit sexual activities with civilians. The war ended when Connery was 15, but it was still a big influence upon him – as it was on many other boys of his generation. Since his encounter with the ATS girl, he couldn't help but notice that there was something about a uniform that made a person look very attractive to the opposite sex. This was one of the reasons why, as he approached 16, he joined the Sea Cadets. When he discovered that he enjoyed the life it offered, he made his first serious career decision. At 16, he joined the Royal Navy.

As it turned out, however, Connery's life was not to be spent on the ocean waves. The exotic promise of a life at sea was not fulfilled by the unglamorous basic training, which took place first at Rosyth and then at a gunnery school. And when Connery eventually went to Portsmouth and to a bunk on HMS *Formidable*, life didn't improve. Not only did he have to work, eat and sleep in cramped quarters with a group of strangers, but he was always being ordered around by a petty officer – not something that an independent youngster like him enjoyed. In fact, just about the only thing he did like were his new tattoos, essential to complete the sailor look. One said 'Mum and Dad', the other 'Scotland Forever'. But he hadn't quite got round to having his personal motto, 'Death Before Dishonour', printed on his arm when his naval career was ended by a series of agonising stomach pains, which put him in hospital for eight weeks. He was eventually diagnosed as having a stomach ulcer: a mixed blessing as, despite the pain, it allowed Connery to be invalided out of a job he had already come to hate.

But what was he to do next with his life? That was the question facing unemployed, 19-year-old Tommy Connery as he returned to Edinburgh. For the next four years, he tried his hand at all sorts of bread-and-butter jobs including coffin polisher, newspaper printer, and artists' model at Edinburgh School of Art. He would stand there in nothing more than a pair of briefs for up to 45 minutes at a time, showing off the muscles built up by attending a weight-lifting club three times a week. It was also a ploy designed to attract girls.

Tommy Connery continued to search for the right career, working as a lorry driver,

cement-mixer, brick-layer and steel-bender.
He helped out backstage at the King's Theatre,
and even received an offer to play football pro-
fessionally for a local club. But what sealed his
fate was a trip to London in 1953, to enter the
UK heats of the Mr Universe competition.

Although he didn't win, all those muscles he
had carefully been acquiring didn't go to
waste. While in London, another Mr
Universe competitor told him that auditions
were being held for the chorus of a new
musical that was about to open. On a whim,
he gate-crashed the auditions and tried out for
a role in *South Pacific*, the story of a Navy nurse
who falls in love with a French planter on an
exotic island. As it happened, the producers
needed beefy, attractive men to play the sailor
members of the chorus. Big Tam was just the

job. Suddenly, care of the Theatre Royal, Drury Lane, he had embarked on a new career: as an actor. And who knew what a humble role in the chorus might lead to?

STARTING OUT

South Pacific was a turning point in Tommy Connery's life in more ways than one. For one thing, it brought him a decent pay packet for the first time in his life. At the age of 24, he was picking up £14 a week 'just for a couple of hours work every evening', as he said. It was more than his father had ever earned.

The role was also behind Tommy's decision to take a new name. What had seemed all right on the streets of Fountainbridge didn't seem quite so suitable for an actor. For a while, Connery had had the nickname Shane (inspired by seeing the Alan Ladd film of that name), and wondered about using that as his Christian name. But in the end, he decided he might as well stick with his second name, Sean, which he had inherited from his grand-father, an Irish tinker who had emigrated to Scotland at the turn of the century. And so it was that he became Sean Connery.

There were other changes too. Now that he was in a different city, and mixing with a whole new kind of people, Connery began to think about the great gaps in his education. 'I was so impressed by actors and how articulate they were,' he says now, 'How much they seemed to know about everything.' Another member of the cast, the actor-director Robert Henderson, encouraged Connery in his decision to start educating himself. He suggested books about acting and plays by Ibsen for Sean to read. Soon the Scotsman was regularly cycling to Chelsea Public Library on a Saturday morning. Doggedly, he made himself plough through novels by Dickens and Thackeray, interspersed with works by Shakespeare. Even when *South Pacific* left London and went on a tour of theatres round the country, Sean carried on with his scheme to educate himself.

Connery had decided that he definitely wanted to be an actor, and he started reading books on dramatic technique – and discussing the contents with Robert Henderson. He would go to other theatres in his spare time to see plays and broaden his horizons. Around the same time, he began studying movement with a teacher called Yat Malmgeren. These lessons would later pay off in a big way. When Connery left the office of Bond producers Cubby Broccoli and Harry Saltzman after his first meeting with them, the two men watched him 'striding like a panther' down the street. The difference between Connery and the other actors who had tried out for the part, Broccoli decided, was like 'comparing a still photograph with a film', and they were convinced he was the right man for the role.

But that was in the future. At that point in time, Connery was still a strolling player, trying to find his feet. He was also enjoying female company among the other cast members of *South Pacific*. His first serious love affair was with an actress called Carol Sopel. Connery fell for her, and they soon became close enough to talk about marriage. But then Carol's parents intervened. Though they liked the young Scotsman, they were completely against the idea of Carol marrying him. Forty years ago, daughters obeyed their parents' wishes more readily than they do now. Carol accepted their view – though very unhappily – and the couple parted.

It took Sean a long time to get over Carol. One night in Dublin, while on tour there, he spent an entire night tramping round the city in the snow, trying to come to terms with his despair. But there were other pretty girls around, and eventually Connery made another romantic attachment: this time to a photographer called Julie Hamilton.

Julie was a different kind of girl. As Sean soon discovered, her mother was Jill Craigie, a director of documentaries and a screenwriter, and her stepfather was Michael Foot, the Labour MP who would later rise to become leader of the Labour Party. They worried about the romance between their daughter, whose pictures were regularly published in the national newspapers, and an actor who seemed to have an uncertain future in front of him. Nonetheless, they too liked the young man. Jill Craigie's contacts meant she could sometimes tip off Sean about possible jobs. To thank her once for doing so, he gave her a puppy, who was christened Vanessa. And from time to time, Sean would sit down to discuss politics with Michael Foot.

When *South Pacific* closed, Sean started going

to auditions, but the rejections were endless. His friend Robert Henderson helped out, offering him occasional parts at Kew Theatre. But work wasn't flooding in. Disappointed, but not deterred, he struggled on with the auditions, and also took the advice of a friend who suggested elocution lessons to tone down his still very thick Scottish accent.

Towards the end of 1956, work began to look up a bit. Connery started getting bit parts in now forgotten films such as *Time Lock* and *Hell Drivers*. Then came a movie called *Action of the Tiger*, in which he had to seduce a young starlet. It wasn't a major role, but there was something about the way he played it that struck the director Terence Young. So much so, that when Connery asked Young at the film's premiere in London if he was going to be a success in it, Young bluntly replied 'No,' then added, 'But keep at it, and one day I'll make it up to you.'

It was in the new medium of television that Sean scored his first big hit. The BBC had started copying the American trend of performing plays live on television and, in 1957, they had plans to broadcast *Requiem for a Heavyweight*, a drama about an American boxer whose career collapses after an eye injury. The original leading man was the American film star Jack Palance. But at the last minute, he had to pull out because a film he was making had run over schedule. The director, Alvin Rakoff, knew Connery: he had given him some small television parts before, and been struck by the young actor's enthusiasm. When Rakoff's wife pointed out that casting him would pull in female as well as male viewers, Connery got the part – even though there was no denying he didn't sound very American.

His accent apart, Connery acted up a storm, and his undoubted virility and sexual magnetism really came through on the screen, despite his nerves at performing the play live. *Requiem for a Heavyweight* was a success and won him encouraging praise from the critics, one of whom even dubbed him a 'British Brando'. By the next day, the phone was ringing in the office of Sean's London agent, and offers of parts started coming in.

One of these was a role in Eugene O'Neill's drama *Anna Christie*, in which Sean was cast opposite a 24-year-old Australian actress called

Diane Cilento, popularly described as a sex-kitten. Sean was captivated by her.

By this time he was living with Julie Hamilton, but he dumped her the instant Diane came on the scene. He went home to their small mews house one day and confessed to Julie that he had fallen for a girl with 'incredible eyes'. Julie got the message, and left, broken-hearted. She had hoped he would marry her, but it was not to be.

Connery now landed a Hollywood film contract with Twentieth Century Fox. He was thrilled, especially when he learned that his first movie, *Another Time, Another Place*, would team him with a real Hollywood star – the 1940's screen siren Lana Turner, known in her heyday as 'The Sweater Girl'. He was cast as a BBC correspondent who has an affair during the Blitz with an American journalist (Lana Turner). The on-screen chemistry between the two inevitably led to rumours that the two were romancing off-screen as well. Lana's obsessively jealous gangster boyfriend Johnny Stompanato ignored the fact that Lana was routinely said to be having an affair with whoever her leading man was. He decided Connery was stealing her away from him and attacked Lana so viciously that he was later deported from Britain, where the film was being made.

Sadly, the excitement of making the film wasn't reflected at the cinema. *Another Time, Another Place* wasn't a very good film, and didn't fare well at the box office. In fact, Fox never succeeded in finding Sean a hit role,

while he turned down some of the parts they
did offer him. The only Hollywood film in
which he really made a mark was a piece of
Americanised Irish blarney called *Darby O'Gill
and the Little People*, which was filmed by
Disney. Fox employed Sean for a while longer,
casting him in a tiny role in the star-studded
war drama, *The Longest Day*, before deciding
they could do without him and releasing him
from his contract.

THE NAME'S BOND –
JAMES BOND

At first sight, James Bond and Sean Connery were worlds apart. One was a commander in the Royal Navy, a man of great sophistication. Connery, on the other hand, was a man whose formal education had ended at 13, and who had left the Navy with the much humbler rank of ordinary seaman. Though he was a good actor, it would still take some coaching to turn him into a convincing *bon vivant*, equally at ease in a casino as when firing a gun.

However, fate seemed to be on Sean's side. When plans to turn Ian Fleming's James Bond novels into films were leaked to the press, the *Daily Express* asked its readers whom they would like to see play 007. The answer was Sean Connery. By coincidence, while producers Harry Saltzman and Albert 'Cubby' Broccoli were buying the rights to the Bond films, Broccoli and his wife happened to watch *Darby O'Gill and the Little People*, and were impressed by Sean's performance.

However, the American studio, United Artists, which was providing the $1 million budget, wanted a bigger name than Sean Connery to star in *Dr No* and had already offered the part to James Mason. Author Ian Fleming suggested that the role should go to the much more upper-crust David Niven.

Broccoli and Saltzman decided to meet Connery for themselves and were immediately struck by his masculinity and immense self-confidence; every time he wanted to make a point, he would slap his thigh or bang on the desk. What's more, he refused point-blank to do a screen test for them, an aggressive and most unusual stance for a comparatively little-known actor to take.

This only made Broccoli and Saltzman keener to have him. They decided he was ideal, even after receiving a telegram from United Artists in New York saying, 'See if you can do better'. Broccoli and Salzman knew they weren't going to do better: they offered the role to Sean, along with a cheque for £6,000. He couldn't believe his luck. Being offered the role of 007, he said, 'was like asking a boy who was crazy about cars if he'd like a Jaguar as a present'.

Director Terence Young – the same director who had spotted Sean a few years earlier during *Action of the Tiger* – started taking Connery in hand. The elegantly-dressed Young was the perfect man to give the rough diamond some polish. He took Connery to his own Savile Row tailor to get him kitted out in the smart suits and dinner jackets that Commander Bond would wear. He also prescribed more elocution lessons to curb the Scottish accent still further. And in one rather extreme measure designed to coach him in Bond's

Sean Connery with Ursula Andress, *Dr No*

style, Young even insisted that Sean sleep in one of the Savile Row suits, complete with shirt and tie. That done, they flew to Jamaica and started work on *Dr No*.

Connery enjoyed making the film, particularly working with the inaugural Bond girl Ursula Andress – whose first appearance in the film, coming out of the sea in a bikini – made its own little bit of cinema history.

But when *Dr No* was finished, United Artists had a sudden panic that the film wasn't good enough. The studio delayed its release by several months, then nervously tried it out at one sneak preview in Los Angeles. Even though the audience response was enthusiastic, they gave it only a limited release in the States, showing it at smaller cinemas and drive-ins. It took a successful premiere and ecstatic reviews in London to convince them they were on to a winner.

In 1962, no one had seen a hero like James Bond before, and the impact on the public of a man – simultaneously sexy, dashing and lethal – was immense. Even the Vatican noticed James Bond, issuing a public statement disapproving of the levels of violence in the film.

The film grew by word of mouth, and queues built up outside every cinema showing *Dr No* (or *No Need for Any Doctors* as it was translated in Japan). There were posters everywhere of Sean Connery as James Bond clutching his gun. The gun was supposed to be Bond's trusty Walther PPK 7.65mm automatic, but in fact was nothing more lethal than a £25 airgun used for killing rabbits and owned by the photographer who shot the poster. It had been hastily pressed into Sean's hand when the real gun failed to materialise for the photo session, and there it stayed.

The success of *Dr No* made a second film about James Bond inevitable. The announcement that it would be called *From Russia with Love* brought fan letters pouring in to Sean from women all over the world, offering him their own love. But they were too late. Sean and Diane had now been together for five years, and were about to seal their relationship. The more experienced actor of the two, she had encouraged and coached Connery. The relationship had had its stormy patches, but in November 1962, after her divorce from

Italian writer Andre Volpe had come through, she and Sean quietly slipped off to Gibraltar and got married.

Sean was already beginning to demonstrate a fierce desire to keep his private life private. He was particularly keen to keep quiet the fact that Diane was now pregnant, and so the marriage took place with the minimum of fuss. He and Diane simply borrowed the services of two local taxi drivers, Gonzalez and Garcia, to witness the ceremony at a Gibraltar register office. And then they went off on honeymoon to Spain.

After the honeymoon, shooting of *From Russia with Love* continued, in a variety of exotic locations including Istanbul. It was to here that Diane came after giving birth to the couple's son, whom they named Jason. He was a half-brother for Diane's own daughter, Giovanna, then aged six.

Connery was delighted to be a father for the first time and eagerly helped look after his new son. However, there were strains in the marriage, and they began to show early. Connery had always hoped to be known as a serious actor – most unusually, when he signed the contract to play 007, he had insisted on being released between Bond films to go off and make other movies. Diane, for all the success of *Dr No*, was continually telling Connery that he was worthy of better things.

From Russia with Love was an even greater success than *Dr No*. Connery now had the honour of being approached by Alfred

With Tippi Hedren in Hitchcock's *Marnie*

Hitchcock, who asked Sean if he would like to be in his new psychological drama, *Marnie*. If Hitchcock expected Connery to leap at the chance, he was wrong. Not only did Connery put in a request for a very hefty fee – £400,000, a huge increase on the £6,000 he had been paid just three years earlier – he also demanded to see the script. Hitchcock was stunned. Cary Grant had never asked to see a script, he told Connery. 'Yes, but I'm not Cary Grant,' Connery replied. Much to everyone's surprise, he got his way.

He had been warned that Hitchcock had a reputation for treating his actors badly, ever since famously announcing that they were 'cattle'. But though the film was not one of Hitch's best, Sean nonetheless enjoyed working with The Master. It gave him a valuable

chance to show that there was more to him
than James Bond, and that he really could act.

Connery then returned to his role as James
Bond. *Goldfinger* would be the most successful
James Bond movie to date. It not only had a
stunning Bond girl – Shirley Eaton – but a
wonderful, gadget-packed car, with machine
guns behind the headlights and an ejector seat.
In many ways, it was the prototype for all the
Bond films to follow, and it inspired a spy
craze on television, spawning shows like *The
Man from U.N.C.L.E.*, and *Our Man Flint*.

Making *Goldfinger* was not a happy experience. On the one hand, Connery was increasingly unhappy at the way that Bond was
taking over his personality. He wanted to be
recognised as an actor, not mistaken for a

fictional spy. On the other, he rowed with the producers over his pay, convinced he was worth more to the James Bond film franchise than he was receiving. He got his salary increase and a share of the profits as well, but it didn't help to smooth his relationship with Broccoli and Saltzman. Broccoli and Saltzman were also beginning to argue among themselves about the way the films were going. Connery would later say: 'They're not exactly enamoured of each other. Probably because they're both sitting on $50 million dollars or pounds, and looking across the desk at each other, and thinking "that beggar's got half of what should be all mine".'

For his own part, Connery – remembering all too clearly those impoverished days in Scotland – was adamant that he should be paid what he felt he was worth. It was a courageous move to tackle the producers of a film, but Connery's view was, 'I'm worth what I get. It's something I learnt as a kid in Scotland: you get damn all for nothing.'

Further cracks began to appear in Connery's marriage. Diane still believed he was capable of much better things, and would say so repeatedly, sometimes in a voice loud enough to be heard by the cast and crew on the *Goldfinger* set.

None of the tensions showed in the film, which had a cracking plot and was released in 1964 to rave reviews and wild public acclaim. It cost only £2 million to make, but made £23 million at the box office in its first year, making it the fastest money-maker in the history of movies at the time.

The film was also responsible for cementing Sean's interest in golf. He had had golf lessons in the past, but now he studied the game with a passion, wanting to make it appear that Bond played golf as well as he did everything else in his life.

Soon golf was an obsession, and he would bet large amounts with his partners on winning: sometimes as much as £100 a hole. This wasn't just reckless extravagance. He had worked hard to make a living, and now he was successful, he was damn well going to enjoy himself. 'Golf, food and drink – those are the things I enjoy,' he said. 'And the only point in having money is to indulge them.'

Diane still wasn't happy, though. Before

Connery came along, she had been quite a well-known actress. But now her identity was being taken over. She wasn't only Mrs Sean Connery, but sometimes Mrs James Bond as well. Outwardly the marriage seemed to be weathering the problems: in interviews Diane talked of how much she and Sean would like to make a film together, if they could just fit space into their diaries.

Diane had eagerly planned for them to go to Australia that year – 1965 – and make a film together. But the arrangements were scotched when the filming of *Thunderball* was brought forward. Diane was so furious at the change in plans that she asked for a trial separation. She got it, and Sean walked out of their home in Acton.

Claudine Auger and Sean Connery on the beach, *Thunderball*

A TIME OF GOODBYES

1965 was not a happy year for Sean Connery. As soon as the press got wind of the fact that he and Diane were having a trial separation, they descended in droves. And what made it worse was that instead of reporting it as a separation between Sean and his wife, the headlines were screaming '007 parts from Diane Cilento'. Once again Sean's personality was buried under that of James Bond, much to his chagrin.

Meanwhile, he was still unhappy about the salary he was receiving. It seemed to him that he was doing all the work, and someone else was getting all the money. By 1965, a glance at the figures showed that while the Bond films had cost $10 million to make, they had raked in 15 times that amount at the box office. It all helped convince Sean that he was still being underpaid, and he went to discuss the situation with Cubby Broccoli and Harry Saltzman. He told them he wanted to renegotiate his fee for the fifth Bond film, *You Only Live Twice*. He wanted a salary of $1 million for the film. At that time, only a handful of other stars were earning that kind of money, including Elizabeth Taylor. But Sean felt he was worth it, especially when an American magazine voted him the most successful movie money-spinner of the year, ahead of Richard Burton and John Wayne. Saltzman and Broccoli refused his request, and his relationship with them became increasingly strained.

It was with these pressures on him that Connery flew out to the Bahamas in April to start work on the fourth James Bond movie, *Thunderball*. Diane Cilento arrived a fortnight after shooting started and stayed for the next seven weeks to try and patch up the marriage. Although outwardly the couple looked happy, colleagues on the set could hear fierce rows between them that went on late into the night.

However, the marriage soldiered on: Diane for one was determined that it should, despite all the pressures on them. She told one reporter: 'This industry can take hold of you and wrap you up like a piece of meat. But I can tell you, we are not going to let ourselves be merchandised. Sean and I have our own lives to lead in our own way.'

They attempted to do so. Sean was still trying to make films that had nothing to do with James Bond, but it seemed that every time he did so, he was doomed to disappointment and frustration. Before making *Thunderball*, he had flown to the Egyptian desert to work on a serious drama called *The Hill*. It was the story of a group of soldiers in a tough military prison, and Sean played a hard-bitten Scots sergeant who leads a rebellion against the appalling conditions there. It received good reviews – of the kind that praised the acting rather the action, which Sean preferred – but it was a box office flop in the States. MGM quietly buried the film in the USA, and

Connery as a hard-bitten sergeant in *The Hill*

although it was nominated for a cluster of British Academy Awards, it had faded from the minds of the American Academy by the time it came to hand out that year's Oscars.

Sean did better on the home front, deciding there would be more chance of privacy for himself and Diane if they left their house in Acton, whose address so many journalists seemed to know. So he put it up for sale and departed for the quiet and comparative privacy of Putney.

However, peace was always going to be hard to find for an actor playing James Bond. Connery was still under contract to make *You Only Live Twice*, which proved to be a deeply unhappy experience. When the cast and crew arrived in Japan to film on location there, Sean was besieged by journalists. One paparazzo was so desperate to prolong an interview with him that he even followed Sean into the gents, much to Sean's fury.

Sean also found that Bond films were taking longer to shoot, and that any characterisation was swamped by all the gadgetry. After six month's work on *You Only Live Twice*, Sean finally decided he had had enough. The frustrations, and his own well-publicised disputes with the directors, led him to announce that he was quitting.

After *You Only Live Twice*, he fulfilled his promise to Diane that he would work with her. He directed, and she and Robert Hardy starred, in a play called *I've Seen You Cut Lemons*. But after a tour in Oxford and Newcastle, it lasted only six weeks in London's West End. Friends saw it as little more than an attempt to patch up the fading relationship.

In public, Diane was still optimistic about their marriage. She had now embarked on a new career as a novelist, and would go off to write at their house in Spain. It was all very cosy, she told interviewers. She would sit at one end of the garden writing, and he would sit at the other reading her manuscript, occasionally coming over to suggest changes. Many years later, however, their son Jason would reveal that this picture of domestic bliss wasn't quite as it seemed. He would hear them arguing from his bedroom, several floors above theirs.

By 1970, there was a new woman in the life of

Sean Connery. Like him, she was married, but that didn't stop it being love at first sight when they first met at a golf tournament in Morocco. Micheline Roquebrune, a petite and sexy French woman, was picking up the ladies' award at the championship, and Sean was picking up the men's. Their eyes met in the club house, Micheline said, 'and as far as I was concerned, it was love at first sight. And I think there was something in return from him too.' There must have been, for the following year Diane moved out of the house in Putney, and Sean appeared on the doorstep to tell reporters that this time the marriage was finally over.

He in turn also left the Putney house and moved into a Chelsea apartment overlooking the river. He was thoroughly tickled by the history of the flat, which had once been

The Anderson Tapes: safe breaking

owned by Ribbentrop, Hitler's ambassador to Britain. Sean would tell anyone who listened that 'five minutes after he moved out of the place, when Hitler called him back to Germany, the neighbours had stolen all the champagne and paintings.'

Connery still found work in films, even though he had abandoned Bond. He made movies like *The Anderson Tapes*, the account of a daring robbery on a block of flats. And then in 1971, he made another daring financial move: Broccoli and Saltzman, who had hired George Lazenby to make *On Her Majesty's Secret Service*, with unhappy results, now came back to Sean and asked if he would sign a contract to make another Bond film. It cost them dear, as this time Sean was in a good position to get what he wanted: a fee of one and a quarter million dollars, plus a percentage of the profits. Sean got his way and then went on to demonstrate that he didn't really need the money by giving it to the Scottish Educational Trust, a new charity set up to help poor Scottish kids get a better chance in life.

This particular 'poor Scottish kid' was now doing very well for himself. A major investor with the private Dunbar bank, he was such a valued customer that they invited him to join the board. How did they treat him when they saw him coming, a journalist once asked. Did they wheel out the red carpet? 'No,' Connery joked, 'they usually cover up the till.' His joke covered his more serious worries about his finances remaining private. By now, he was starting to negotiate a divorce settlement with

007 again in *Diamonds are Forever*

Diane Cilento, and he was determined that the details of their agreement should be confidential and hidden from the prying eyes of the press.

'PATIENCE IS A VIRTUE'

In 1972, while Connery was making a film called *The Offence*, his father died. Connery was deeply shaken, as he had always been close to his dad. Moreover, Joe's death from cancer was so sudden, said Connery, that it 'brought me up with a tremendous jolt.' One year Joe had come away from the medical with his doctor with a clean bill of health; the next, the x-rays had shown he had cancer. Sean had gone to Edinburgh to discuss treatment with

Joe's doctor, but had been told there was no hope.

'Now he's dead, and it's a more sobering experience than I thought it would be,' Connery said. 'The Masai tribe say that you're not a man until your father dies. They may be right. But if it's true, it's a pretty stiff price to pay.'

Sean had to pick himself up and carry on, but Joe's death was not the only change in his life. This was also the year he said goodbye – finally, or so he thought – to another major influence on his life: James Bond. Roger Moore had now been signed to play 007 in the eighth Bond film, *Live and Let Die*. The producers told Sean that they would willingly have him back, but he refused.

Murder on the Orient Express, Sean Connery and
Vanessa Redgrave

Bond's absence left an undeniable gap in Connery's life. His agent, Denis Selinger, told him simply to make as many films as possible. He knew that Sean's film roles away from Bond had often satisfied him, even though they had rarely done well at the box office. So he reminded Sean that big stars of the 1940s and 1950s had often made two or three movies a year, in the hope that the more films they churned out, the greater the chance that one of them would be a hit.

Sean took Selinger's advice, but he still struggled to establish himself away from the shadow of Bond. For every success, like the star-studded Agatha Christie film *Murder on the Orient Express*, there was a flop like *Zardoz*, a strange futuristic film about a time when people never die.

Friends Caine and Connery in *The Man Who Would Be King*

Away from the screen, Sean was now spending more time in Spain. He bought a tumbledown villa near Marbella, and began converting it into a luxury home, with a study for him, and a studio where Micheline could paint. In public, he still denied that he and Micheline would get married. He kept the press guessing about his plans even after his divorce from Diane was finalised in October 1973.

But finally, Sean and Micheline did wed: and once again, in secret. In 1975, they quietly married in Gibraltar, but Sean didn't tell the press until over four months later.

The same year, Sean made *The Man Who Would Be King*, the story of two soldiers who swindle their way into becoming the rulers of

Sean and his wife, Micheline

a small Indian kingdom. It teamed Connery
with his great friend Michael Caine, who
enjoyed the fun they had together, even
though they were stuck in a 'dumb little town'
on the edge of the Sahara Desert. There
wasn't much to do at nights except to go to
the local disco, and even that lost some of its
attractions because the only dancers were
men: women weren't allowed out at night.
Caine and Connery were standing at the bar
one night when Connery leant over and joked
to his friend: 'Do you mind if I dance with
your driver? Mine's too ugly.'

Connery adored making the film, and it did
well at the box office too. So well, in fact, that
he decided to sue the studio that made it,
Allied Artists, for underpaying him. Accord-
ing to the studio, the film still wasn't making

Never Say Never Again, Kim Basinger and Connery on the dance floor

enough for Sean to be paid the share of the profits that he was owed. Caine sued too. It was a tough and risky financial battle but the actors won: Allied Artists went bankrupt. 'And quite right too,' said Connery, adding that for the money they had paid him, they deserved only to get 'The Men Who Would Be Prince'.

The 1970s became the 1980s and Connery now had a long string of films behind him, most of them far from brilliant. Perhaps that was why, in 1983, he allowed Micheline to talk him into making a new Bond film. Unlike Diane, Micheline loved seeing Sean as Bond. She even came up with the title for the 1983 movie – *Never Say Never Again*. She also found his co-star, after spotting a knock out blonde who was staying at London's Grosvenor

House hotel and following her to her room. The blonde turned out to be Kim Basinger.

Another beauty in the film was actress Barbara Carrera, who had a love scene with Sean. Normally, Micheline tried to stay away when these were being filmed, but one day she made a mistake and walked onto the *Never Say Never Again* set just in time to see her husband and Barbara romping for the cameras. Micheline was hideously embarrassed and wanted to run away, but it occurred to her that the film crew would all gossip if she looked noticeably upset. So she forced herself to sit down and watch a while, before coolly getting up and sauntering away.

All in all, *Never Say Never Again* was a hard film to make. By the end of shooting, Connery was

The Name of the Rose, medieval sleuths Connery and Christian Slater

so drained and disenchanted that he didn't make any movies for the next two years. To add to his melancholy, in April 1985 his beloved mother Effie died. Sean returned to Scotland to join his brother Neil at the funeral.

In 1986, Sean's career famine ended with a bang. After rejecting many scripts, he suddenly agreed to make *Highlander*, a strange film about an immortal time traveller. Against all the odds, it went on to become a cult hit. He then made the medieval thriller, *The Name of the Rose*, in which, as a cowled monk, he and young heart-throb Christian Slater investigated a string of murders at an Italian monastery.

The story puzzled the Americans so much

that they stayed away from the cinema. But in Europe, it was a smash hit, pulling in $100 million. Suddenly Sean's career was back on track, a fact confirmed by his next role in *The Untouchables*. Kevin Costner, as 1920s' mafia hunter Eliot Ness, was nominally the star, but Connery stole the show with his performance as the ageing maverick Irish cop, Malone. His lines on how to trap wanted mob boss Al Capone: 'He puts one of yours in the hospital, you put one of his in the morgue,' were soon being as widely quoted by film fans as the words, 'The name's Bond – James Bond', had been 20 years earlier.

The Untouchables put Connery back at the top of his profession, and won him an Oscar as Best Supporting Actor – the first time he had

Sean and Kevin Costner, *The Untouchables*

won this coveted prize. Reflecting how long it had taken him to be recognised by the film industry, he climbed the stairs to the Oscar podium and told the star-studded crowd, 'Patience is a virtue'.

The role of Malone finally helped put Sean's career into a new category. At last, he had shaken off the ghost of James Bond and become a senior star: one who was still fit and good-looking enough to be able to conduct believable romances with beautiful women – as he did with Michelle Pfeiffer in the John Le Carré spy film, *The Russia House*.

Connery also brought gravitas and the natural authority of the older man to his work. Film characters never messed with James Bond without learning that he carried a gun and was

Connery as King Arthur greets Richard Gere as Lancelot, *First Knight*

With Michele Pfeiffer in the Le Carré spy film, *The Russia House*

prepared to use it, now they knew not to mess with Connery because he was a senior figure who commanded respect.

He made a convincing submarine commander in *The Hunt for Red October*, and an equally convincing King Richard in another Kevin Costner film, *Robin Hood: Prince of Thieves*. Kingship suited him so well that when he went to play King Arthur, to Richard Gere's Lancelot, in *First Knight*, even the director was in awe of him. 'It was as much as I could do not to go down on one knee and call him Sire,' Jerry Zucker said afterwards.

Sean's seniority is reflected in some of the awards he has now received. There were honorary degrees from Scottish universities, and in

1991 he received the Freedom of the City of Edinburgh.

Although he is now eligible for a quiet retirement and a free bus pass he is, he says, busier than ever. He and Clint Eastwood – a golf fanatic after Sean's own heart – talk regularly about making a golf movie. And the man who started his life in great poverty is apparently too afraid of returning to it to give up. Just before his 65th birthday, he said he wouldn't quit 'because I can't afford to'. In January 1996, when he received a lifetime achievement prize at the Golden Globe awards, Connery added: 'I'll do everything I can to deserve this, except retire.'

But whether or not he goes on acting, he has one ambition left: 'I suppose more than anything else I'd like to be an old man with a good face, like Hitchcock or Picasso,' he says. 'They know life is not just a popularity contest.'

FILMOGRAPHY

The year refers to the first release date
of the film

1956 No Road Back
1957 Hell Drivers
1957 Time Lock
1957 Action of the Tiger
1958 Another Time, Another Place
1959 Darby O'Gill and the Little People
1959 Tarzan's Greatest Adventure
1961 Frightened City
1961 On the Fiddle
1962 The Longest Day

Sean Connery

1962	Dr No
1963	From Russia with Love
1964	Marnie
1964	Woman of Straw
1964	Goldfinger
1965	The Hill
1965	Thunderball
1966	A Fine Madness
1967	You Only Live Twice
1968	Shalako
1970	The Molly Maguires
1971	The Red Tent
1971	The Anderson Tapes
1971	Diamonds Are Forever
1973	The Offence
1974	Zardoz
1974	Murder on the Orient Express
1975	Ransom (aka The Terrorists)
1975	The Wind and the Lion

1975	The Man Who Would Be King
1976	Robin and Marian
1976	The Next Man
1977	A Bridge Too Far
1978	The First Great Train Robbery
1979	Meteor
1979	Cuba
1981	Outland
1981	Time Bandits
1982	Five Days One Summer
1982	The Man with the Deadly Lens
	(aka Wrong is Right)
1983	Sword of the Valiant
1983	Never Say Never Again
1986	The Name of the Rose
1986	Highlander
1987	The Untouchables
1988	The Presidio
1988	Memories of Me

ACKNOWLEDGEMENTS

Allied Artists (courtesy Kobal)
Aquarius
Columbia (courtesy Kobal)
Kobal Collection
MGM/7Arts (courtesy Kobal)
Neue Constantin/ZDF (courtesy Kobal)
Paramount (courtesy Kobal)
Pathé/MGM (courtesy Kobal)
UA/Eon/Dan Jaq (courtesy Kobal)
United Artists (courtesy Kobal)
Universal (courtesy Kobal)
Warner Bros (courtesy Kobal)